SPORT BIKE Racing

The Thrill of Racing

LEE-ANNE T. SPALDING

Rourke
Publishing LLC
Vero Beach, Florida 32964

www.rourkepublishing.com

PHOTO CREDITS: © Kreusch: page 5; © Yamaha Media: page 8; © Nildo Scoop: page 10, © Keith Robinson: page 12; © Eric Gevaert: page 13; © Zhorov Igor Vladimirovich: page 14; © Marcel Jancovic: page 14; © Michael Stokes: page 16; © Maj. William Thurmond: page 17; © Suzuki Media: page 18; © digitalsport-photoagency: page 20, 22

Edited by Meg Greve

Cover design by Tara Raymo
Interior design by Teri Intzegian

Library of Congress Cataloging-in-Publication Data

Spalding, Lee-Anne T.

  Sport bike racing / Lee-Anne T. Spalding.
     p. cm. -- (The thrill of racing)
  Includes index.
  ISBN 978-1-60472-374-8 (hardcover)
  ISBN 978-1-60472-811-8 (softcover)
  1. Motorcycles, Racing--Juvenile literature. 2. Motorcycles--Juvenile
literature. I. Title.
  GV1060.S59 2008

  796.7'5--dc22

                    2008012593

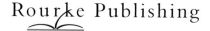

Rourke Publishing

www.rourkepublishing.com – rourke@rourkepublishing.com
Post Office Box 3328. Vero Beach. FL 32964

Table of Contents

The road! The wind! The metal! The speed! Although motorcycles have been around since the late 1800s, the first true racing motorcycles, or sport bikes, came much later. Vincent Motorcycles designed bikes for speed in the 1920s, but the true design for racing motorcycles took another forty years to develop.

Vincent Black Lightning motorcycle

SOME SPORT BIKE FIRSTS

1949
Vincent's
Black Lightning

1968
Triumph's
Trident

1969
Honda's
CB750

1972
Kawasaki's
Z 1

1974
Ducati's
750 Sport

1977
Suzuki's
RN400

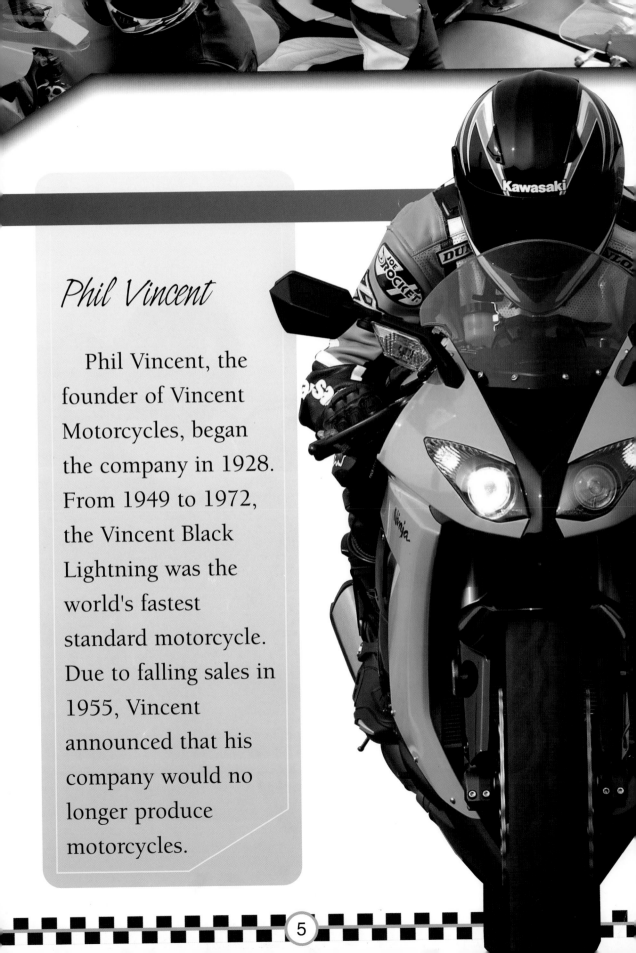

Phil Vincent

Phil Vincent, the founder of Vincent Motorcycles, began the company in 1928. From 1949 to 1972, the Vincent Black Lightning was the world's fastest standard motorcycle. Due to falling sales in 1955, Vincent announced that his company would no longer produce motorcycles.

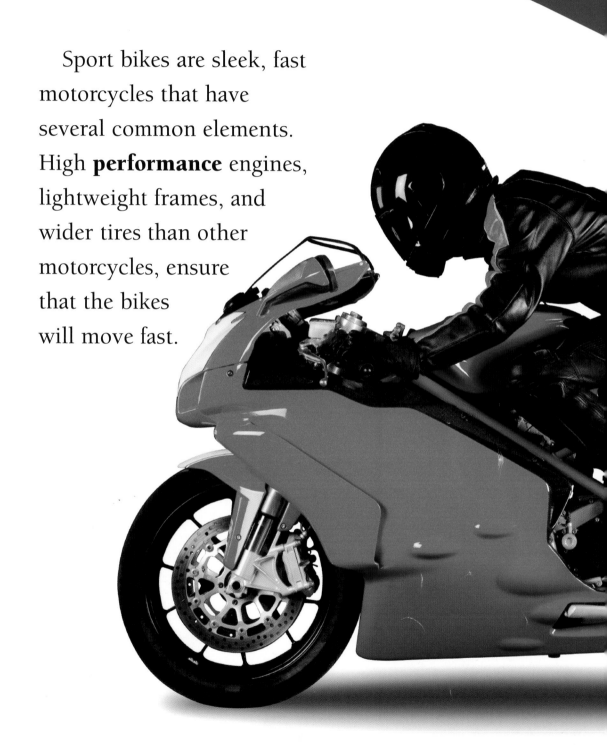

Sport bikes are sleek, fast motorcycles that have several common elements. High **performance** engines, lightweight frames, and wider tires than other motorcycles, ensure that the bikes will move fast.

Sport bike riders drive on regular roads and highways, too. Due to the overall design of the sport bike, riders must lean over the tank while riding. This position allows them and the bikes to be **aerodynamic**.

A Safe Ride

Safe and **responsible** sport bike riders wear helmets, goggles, jackets, pants, gloves, and boots while taking their motorcycle for a ride.

True road racing occurs when riders or spectators **temporarily** close a road for racing. These types of road races do not occur as much as they once did due to concerns for the safety of the riders and the public.

The Isle of Man Tourist Trophy Race is one of the most famous true road race events. Beginning in 1907, this race took place in the British Isles. Riders rode their sport bikes at speeds around **120 mph (193 km/h)**. In 1976, the last true Isle of Man road race took place.

You Asked...

Who was the very first winner of the Isle of Man?

*Charlie Collier was the overall winner of the first event with a time of 4 hours 8 minutes and 8 seconds. His average speed throughout the race was only 38 **mph** (61 **km/h**).*

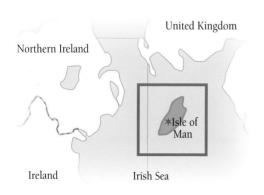

United Kingdom

Northern Ireland

*Isle of Man

Ireland

Irish Sea

Motorcycle Grand Prix (Moto GP) refers to the highest level of motorcycle road racing. Riders participate in one of three different classes of racing determined by the bike's engine size: **125 cc, 250 cc, and Moto GP**. Moto GP is the top class of motorcycle road racing.

Valentino Rossi

In 1979, Valentino Rossi was born in Italy. To date, he is one of the best motorcycle racers of all time having won seven Grand Prix World Championship titles.

Currently, 18 Moto GP events take place each year in 16 different countries. In 2008, a Moto GP event took place at the Indianapolis Motor Speedway, home of the famous car racing event, the Indianapolis 500.

Countries with Road Racing Events

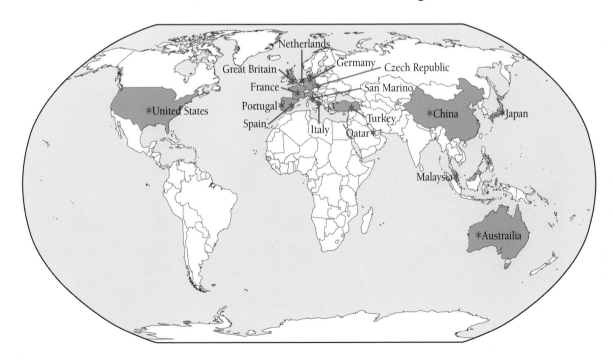

Motocross is much like road racing except it takes place on off-road racetracks. Up to forty riders start the race at the same time. The surface of the tracks may be sand, mud, or grass. They also include hills and jumps where riders become airborne.

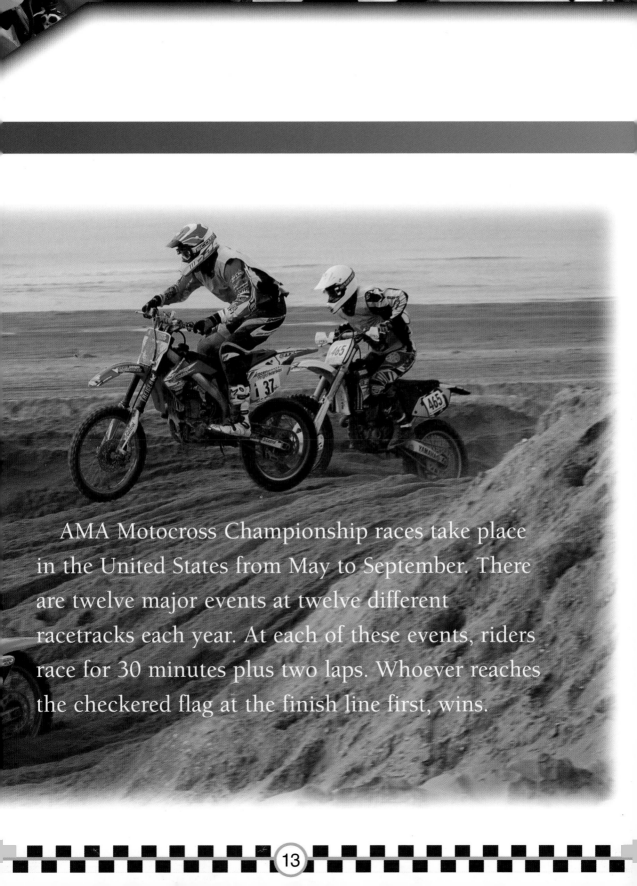

AMA Motocross Championship races take place in the United States from May to September. There are twelve major events at twelve different racetracks each year. At each of these events, riders race for 30 minutes plus two laps. Whoever reaches the checkered flag at the finish line first, wins.

Track racing is where an **individual** or team races around an oval track. There are different types of track races depending upon the surface of the track. It could be dirt, asphalt, or even ice.

The most common type of track racing is speedway racing. Riders race on dirt tracks. The dirt allows the rider to powerslide around the curves of the track at high speeds. Four to six riders race around the track at least four times to the finish line.

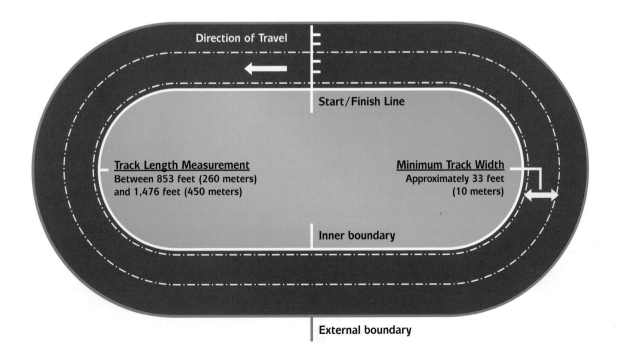

Direction of Travel

Start/Finish Line

Track Length Measurement
Between 853 feet (260 meters)
and 1,476 feet (450 meters)

Minimum Track Width
Approximately 33 feet
(10 meters)

Inner boundary

External boundary

Drag Racing

Drag races are only for two riders at a time. Racers line up at the start line and race down a quarter mile paved track, also called a drag strip. Whoever reaches the finish line first, wins.

You Asked...

What are the lights called that signal the beginning of a drag race?

The Christmas tree featuring red, yellow, and green lights signal drivers when to begin.

The most popular form of drag racing is the pro stock bike **category**. This type of racing has been around since the 1980s. Racing motorcycles **sprint** to the end of the drag strip where they slow down in the shutdown area.

NHRA stands for the National Hot Rod Association.

The American Motorcycle Association (AMA) is the largest motorsports **organization** in the world. The professional racing of motorcycles became so popular that AMA Pro Racing formed in 1994.

AMA Pro Racing holds more than eighty professional events each year. Among them, the most popular events are the AMA Superbike Series that include the AMA Supercross, AMA Motocross, and AMA Superbike Championship.

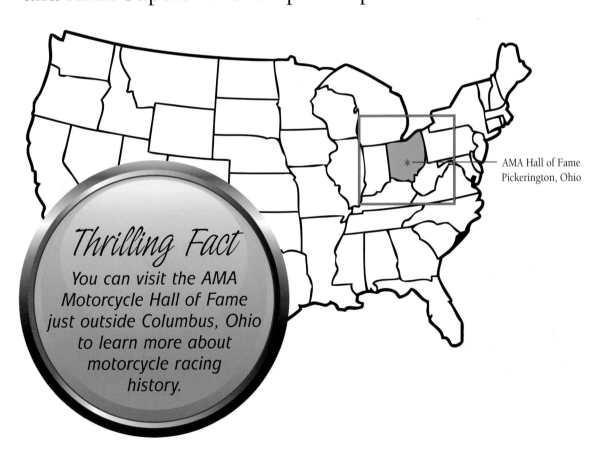

AMA Hall of Fame
Pickerington, Ohio

Thrilling Fact

You can visit the AMA Motorcycle Hall of Fame just outside Columbus, Ohio to learn more about motorcycle racing history.

Show Me the Money

When first produced, early sport bikes were several hundred dollars. Today, sport bikes, the safety equipment, and the special modifications made to individual sport bikes are expensive.

Sport Bike Bills

Sport Bike Make & Model	Price (2008)
Kawasaki Ninja 650R	$6,499
Yamaha YZ450F	$7,199
Honda Interceptor	$10,799
Suzuki Hayabusa	$11,999

Thrilling Fact

The introductory price of the Honda CB750 produced in 1969 was only $1,495.

The Last Lap

Sport bikes and racing events have been around for a long time. Riders race on paved roads, dirt, grass, oval tracks, and even over man made jumps all over the world. There is no doubt that sport bike racing and their events are quite a thrill!

Glossary

aerodynamic (air-oh-dye-NAM-mik): designed to move through the air very easily and quickly

category (KAT-uh-gor-ee): a class or group of things

cc (SEE-SEE): abbreviation for cubic centimeters; the higher the number, the more powerful the engine

individual (in-duh-VIJ-oo-uhl): single and separate

km/h (KAY EM AYCH): abbreviation for kilometers per hour

mph (EM PEE AYCH): abbreviation for miles per hour

organization (or-guh nuh-ZAY-shuhn): a number of people joined together for a particular purpose

performance (pur-FOR-muhnss): a public presentation

responsible (ri-SPON-suh-buhl): having or involving important duties

sprint (SPRINT): a very fast race run over a short distance

temporarily (TEM-puh-rer-ihl-ee): lasts for only a short time

Index

Websites to Visit

www.motorcyclemuseum.org

http://en.wikipedia.org/wiki/Motorcycle_racing

www.amadirectlink.com/roadride

Further Reading

Dayton, Connor. *Dirt Bikes (Motorcycles: Made for Speed)*.
    PowerKids Press, 2007.

Gifford, Clive. *Racing: The Ultimate Motorsports*.
    Encyclopedia. Kingfisher, 2006.

Woods, Bob. *Hottest Motorcycles (Wild Wheels!)*.
    Enslow Publishers, 2007.

About the Author

Lee-Anne Trimble Spalding is a former public school educator and is currently instructing preservice teachers at the University of Central Florida. She lives in Oviedo, Florida with her husband, Brett and two sons, Graham and Gavin.